A Note to Parents

DK READERS is a compelling new program for beginning readers, designed in conjunction with leading literacy experts, including Dr. Linda Gambrell, Director of the School of Education at Clemson University. Dr. Gambrell has served on the Board of Directors of the International Reading Association and as President of the National Reading Conference.

Beautiful illustrations and superb full-color photographs combine with engaging, easy-to-read stories to offer a fresh approach to each subject in the series. Each DK READER is guaranteed to capture a child's interest while developing his or her reading skills, general knowledge, and love of reading.

The four levels of DK READERS are aimed at different reading abilities, enabling you to choose the books that are exactly right for your child:

Level 1: Beginning to read
Level 2: Beginning to read alone
Level 3: Reading alone
Level 4: Proficient readers

The "normal" age at which a child begins to read can be anywhere from three to eight years old, so these levels are intended only as a general guideline.

No matter which level you select, you can be sure that you are helping your child learn to read, then read to learn!

LONDON, NEW YORK, MUNICH,
MELBOURNE, AND DELHI

Editor Dawn Sirett
Art Editor Jane Horne

Senior Editor Linda Esposito
Senior Art Editor
Diane Thistlethwaite
US Editor Regina Kahney
Production Melanie Dowland
Picture Researcher Angela Anderson
Jacket Designer Simon Oon
Natural History Consultant
Theresa Greenaway

Reading Consultant
Linda B. Gambrell, Ph.D.

First American Edition, 1999
13 14 15 16
Published in the United States by DK Publishing
345 Hudson Street, New York, New York 10014
022-KP824-Nov/1999

Published in Great Britain by Dorling Kindersley Limited
Eyewitness Readers™ is a trademark of Dorling Kindersley Limited, London

Library of Congress Cataloging-in-Publication Data
Wallace, Karen.
    Busy buzzy bee / by Karen Wallace. -- 1st American ed.
    p.   cm. -- (Eyewitness readers)
    Summary: Explains the behavior and lives of bees, discussing how
they collect nectar from flowers, care for their eggs and queen bee,
and communicate with each other.
    ISBN-13:   978-0-7894-4759-3 (plc)
    ISBN-13:   978-0-7894-4758-6 (pb)
    1. Honeybee Juvenile literature. 2. Bees Juvenile literature.
[1. Honeybee.   2. Bees.]   I. Title.   II. Series.
QL568. A6W34   1999
595.79'9 --dc21   99-23160
                                                        CIP
                                                        AC
Color reproduction by Colourscan, Singapore
Printed and bound in China by L.Rex

The publisher would like to thank the following for
their kind permission to reproduce their photographs:
Key: t=top, b=bottom, l=left, r=right, c=center
Bruce Coleman Ltd: Hans Reinhard 7, 28–29, Jane Burton 20–21,
John Shaw 10–11, Kim Taylor front cover b, 14–15; **Environmental
Images**: Vanessa Miles 6 tr; **NHPA**: Jean-Louis LeMoigne 8 t,
Stephen Dalton front cover tl, back cover tl, back cover tr, 11 tr,
16 t, 22 t, 23 r, 24–25; **Oxford Scientific Films**: David Thompson
4–5, 5 tr, 17 b, 18 t, 32 tl, 32 crb, Scott Camazine 18–19; **Planet
Earth Pictures**: Lythgoe 6 b, Richard Coomber 26–27; **Science
Photo Library**: Eye of Science 10 tr, 32 clb; ©**Jerry Young**: 30–31.
Additional photography for DK: Geoff Brightling, Jane Burton, Geoff Dann,
Frank Greenaway, Stephen Oliver, and Kim Taylor.
All other images © Dorling Kindersley Limited
For further information see: www.dkimages.com

Discover more at
www.dk.com

DK READERS

BEGINNING
TO READ
1

Busy Buzzy Bee

Written by Karen Wallace

DK
DK Publishing

Busy Bee has work to do.
She crawls out of her hive.

hive

She spreads her wings.
Busy Bee is looking for a flower.

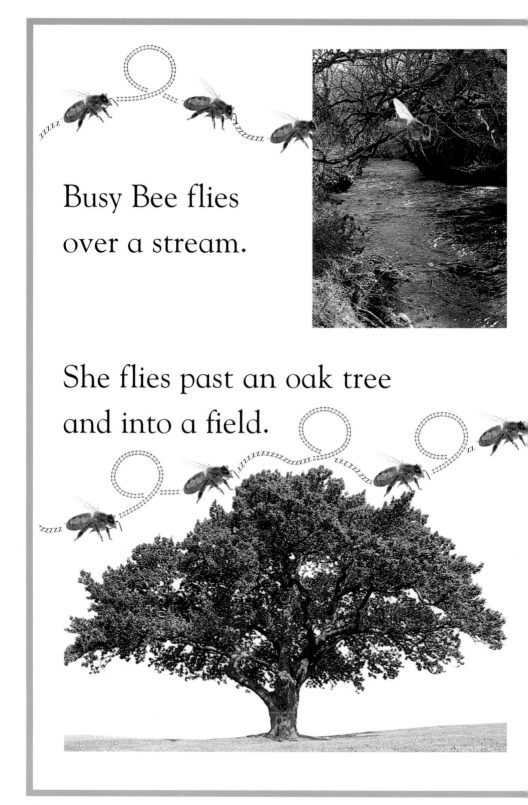

Busy Bee flies
over a stream.

She flies past an oak tree
and into a field.

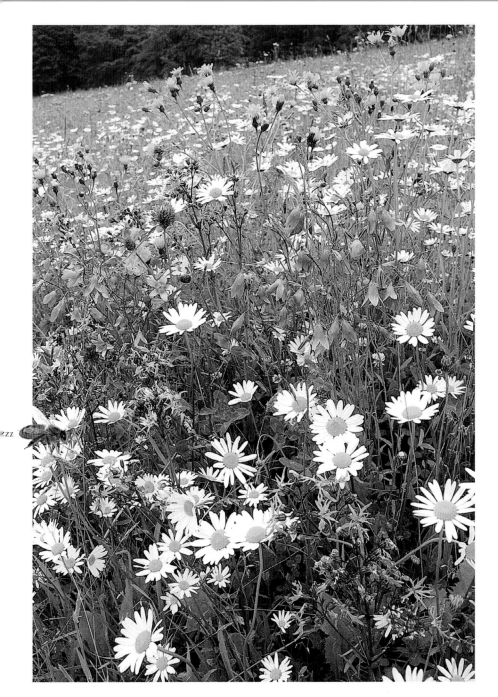

The field is full of wild flowers.

Busy Bee lands on a flower.

Each flower holds
sweet drops of nectar.
Bees make nectar
into honey.
Nectar and honey
are food for bees.

Busy Bee laps up the nectar
with her long, narrow tongue
to take back to the hive.

nectar

Each flower holds
grains of pollen.
Flower pollen is
food for bees, too.

pollen

The pollen sticks
to Busy Bee's
furry body.

She brings it to the hive
on her two back legs.

Busy Bee is a worker bee.

Inside the hive,
there are thousands like her.
All worker bees are female.

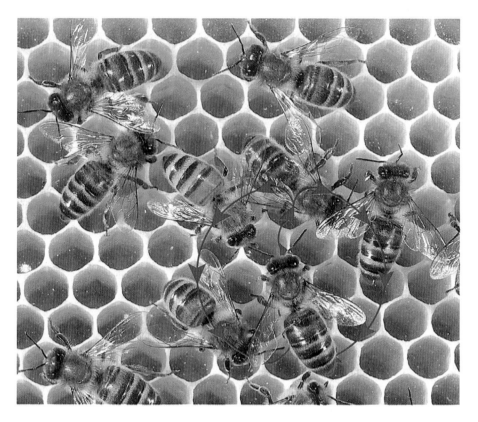

Busy Bee dances a dance.

She waggles her bottom.

She crawls in circles.

Her dance shows
the other workers
the way to find
the flower nectar.

Inside the hive,
the bees make cells.

cell

Some are for the honey
the bees make from nectar.

honey cell   pollen cell

Some are for the pollen
the bees have collected.

Some are for the eggs
that the queen bee lays.

egg cell

Busy Bee has work to do.
First she feeds
the drone bees.

All drones are male.
The drones mate
with a queen bee.

drone

Then Busy Bee
feeds the queen bee.
The queen bee lays
a thousand eggs
every day.

queen
bee

Inside their cells,
the eggs hatch
into bee grubs.

bee grub

Busy Bee and
thousands like her
take some pollen
mixed with honey.
They feed it to
the hungry grubs.

Busy Bee has work to do.
She feeds the bee grubs
every day.

When the grubs are nine days old
she seals their cells
with waxy covers.

Inside their cells,
the bee grubs change.
They grow legs and wings.
They grow long, narrow tongues.

In twelve days
they change from
grubs to bees.

They crawl out and wait
for their new wings to dry.

Busy Bee and thousands like her
touch the young bees
with their feelers.

feelers

They make them welcome
in the hive.
They feed them honey
from the cells.

Busy Bee has work to do.
The young bees are hungry.
Where can she find
more flower nectar?

Where can
she find more
flower pollen?

27

Look!
Another bee is dancing!
She's found a garden
full of flowers.

She waggles her bottom.
She crawls in circles.
Her dance shows Busy Bee
how to find the garden.

Busy Bee and thousands like her fly from the hive.

They find the garden
full of flowers.
They drink the nectar.
They take the pollen.
Busy Bee has work to do.

Picture Word List

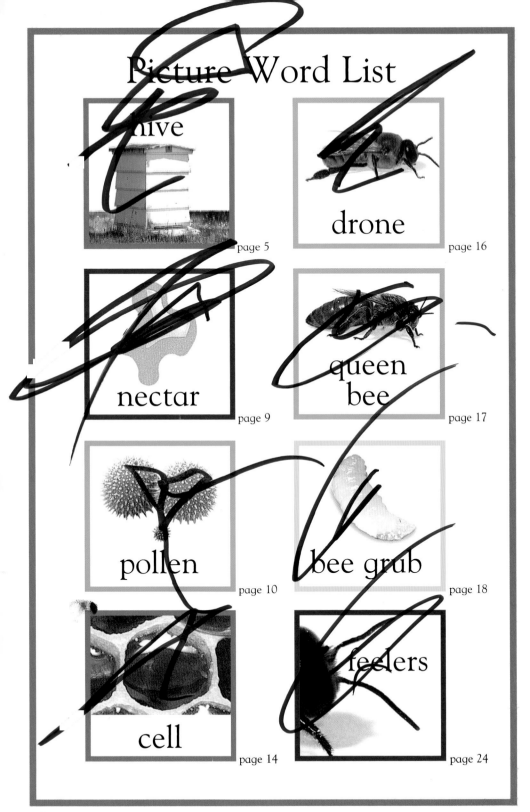

hive
page 5

drone
page 16

nectar
page 9

queen bee
page 17

pollen
page 10

bee grub
page 18

cell
page 14

feelers
page 24

32